THE BEATITUDES

Becoming Citizens
of the Kingdom

CONTENTS

Using This Small Group Resource   4

Session 1: The Poor in Spirit   6

Session 2: Those Who Mourn   12

Session 3: The Meek   18

Session 4: The Righteous and Merciful   24

Session 5: The Pure in Heart   30

Session 6: The Peacemakers   36

Session 7: The Persecuted   42

USING THIS SMALL GROUP RESOURCE

1. Before you begin to prepare for the first session, take a look at the entire study. This will enable you to:

- Understand the direction of each session and the overall purpose of the study.

- Know what your students will be reading and studying each week.

- Begin to think about what you would like to accomplish with this study.

2. Before you teach each session:

- Read over the session guide for that particular week. Doing so will help you become familiar with questions, activities, options, and so on.

- Gather any needed materials.

- Pray for God's direction.

THE SESSIONS

Each session contains:

- *Opener*—An activity or questions that will help get your students thinking about the topic you will be discussing

- *Opening the Word*—The Bible study portion of the session

- *Understanding*—The opportunity for the group to understand how the truth discovered during the session applies to their lives

- *Reflection*—A time for students to reflect individually on what they have learned and how it applies to their experience and world, followed by the invitation to share and discuss

- *Takeaway Thought*—A send-off or challenge for the students to apply what they have learned to their lives

- *Student Handout*—A reproducible handout that each student can use to engage and reflect during the session

INVOLVE EVERYONE

We have designed the questions and activities to enable everyone to participate. Here are some things to keep in mind as you lead your small group:

1. Students are more interested when they are participants rather than spectators.

2. They will remember more of what they discuss and do together than what is said to them.

3. When students get involved in a discussion, be affirming and encouraging.

4. Don't force anyone to participate, but do make sure everyone knows that their input is welcome.

5. Pray for each student in the session, asking God that each one might benefit from the study. Pray for yourself, asking God to assist you as you lead.

SESSION 1:
THE POOR IN SPIRIT

SESSION SNAPSHOT

Weekly Verses: Matthew 5:1-3; James 4:1-8

Session Objective: To help students understand that being "poor in spirit" is good news about God's grace.

OPENER

Invite your students to respond to the following questions.

Would you rather:

- Be a famous athlete or musician?

- Visit 100 years in the past or 100 years in the future?

- Be invisible or read minds?

- Not use your computer for a month or not eat junk food for a month?

- Have to sing instead of speaking or have to dance everywhere you go?

- Have only two close friends or many acquaintances?

- Be rich or poor?

Follow up this activity by saying, "Compared to the others, the last question wasn't very difficult to answer, was it? Today we're talking about Jesus' words, 'Blessed are the poor in spirit.' At first glance, his statement can seem challenging. However, Jesus is bringing us wonderful news about trusting the Father and depending on God's grace. His words are freeing and meant to save us from our self-reliance and striving."

Understanding Matthew 5:1-3

Jesus chose his words carefully as he began his Sermon on the Mount. He said, "Blessed are the poor in spirit, for theirs is the kingdom of heaven" (v. 3). But how can anyone who can claim the kingdom of heaven be "poor" in anything? The first beatitude signals a radical departure from the way the world thinks. If being poor means having no resources to help oneself, then being poor in spirit includes those who recognize they are spiritually helpless. It's referring to people who know they have no way to save themselves. Only those who recognize that they are poor in spirit will realize that they are totally dependent on God.

In a world that tells us to earn more, try harder, and be better, Jesus gives us permission to be honest about our frail humanity—and receive his free, transforming grace.

Understanding James 4:1-8

In chapter four, James warns his fellow believers to submit to God and not the influences of the world (v. 4). He calls out those who are quarreling in church and seeking their own way instead of godly wisdom. *Don't be friends with the world*, he warns, *because that is in opposition to God.*

James is talking to believers who are followers of God and at the same time captivated by the ways of the world. Pride leads us down a path of self-centeredness; however, God "favors the humble." The remedy for pride is submitting to God—turning our focus off self and, in humility, surrendering our will to God.

OPENING THE WORD

Ask a student to read Matthew 5:1-3.

Share with students that in Jesus' day, those with material wealth were viewed as blessed beyond others. The reverse of this belief was that the poor were bad and deserved their poverty. When Jesus said, "Blessed are the poor in spirit," his words would have shocked those who were listening. And yet, he was teaching us about humility, relationship, and trusting the Father. If being poor means having no resources to help oneself, then being poor in spirit means recognizing that we are spiritually helpless and have no way of saving ourselves. Only when we recognize we are poor in spirit do we realize we are totally dependent on God. For Jesus, blessing is all about relationship. That relationship is an invitation into his kingdom.

Discuss the following questions:

- What do you think it means to be poor in spirit?

- How does being poor in spirit bring us into deeper relationship with God?

- In a society so focused on self and consuming more, what are the challenges of remaining poor in spirit?

- In what areas are you tempted to do life in your own strength and without God's help?

Ask a student to read James 4:1-8. Discuss the following questions:

- According to verses 2-3, how important are our motives when we pray?

- In what ways is the world opposed to the ways of God?

- What do you think it means when Scripture says, "He jealously longs for the spirit he has caused to dwell in us" (verse 5)?

- Verse 8 says, "Come near to God and he will come near to you." How does pride keep us away from God? What are the spiritual benefits of a humble spirit?

UNDERSTANDING THE LARGER STORY

Read the following to your students.

Everything God does is for our good. When he invites us to be poor in spirit (depending on him) rather than proud (depending on ourselves), we can trust that he's giving us insight into the best and most fruitful way to live.

So, what are the ways we proudly try to do things on our own? One way is through striving and religious self-help. It's a worldly kind of pride that is nothing new. In Jesus' time, people would work themselves into a frenzy trying to please the gods and goddesses of their day. They would bring elaborate gifts to pagan temples, seeking to "buy" divine favor. Even parts of Judaism were like this. The Sadducees and Pharisees advocated careful observance of Temple liturgy, rituals, and worship. It seemed as though everyone was trying to earn their way, which isn't altogether different from today. Even those who don't strive for God's approval strive for the approval of their peers.

With the first beatitude, Jesus swept away all other approaches to salvation that relied on human strength, smarts, and righteousness. The truth is, God is the source of all, and we must come to him with humble hearts.

REFLECTION

Have students use their student handout for the following activity.

Being poor in spirit is recognizing our need for God. Those areas where we feel the weakest, the most helpless, or ashamed are actually opportunities to draw near to God and rely on his strength. In this way, God turns the bad into good! After explaining this, ask students to find a place to pray and reflect on areas where they need God's help. Invite students to write down the top five things they are depending on the Lord for. If they struggle to come up with answers, they can use the prompts on their student handout.

TAKEAWAY THOUGHT

This week invite students to pray that the Lord will reveal one area in their life where they may be hanging on to pride or self-reliance. When God reveals an issue, tell students to lay it at the foot of the cross and rejoice, knowing they can depend on him to provide for every area of their life.

SESSION 1:
THE POOR IN SPIRIT

 ## THIS WEEK'S SCRIPTURE PASSAGES

Matthew 5:1-3
Now when Jesus saw the crowds, he went up on a mountainside and sat down. His disciples came to him, and he began to teach them. He said: "Blessed are the poor in spirit, for theirs is the kingdom of heaven."

James 4:1-8
What causes fights and quarrels among you? Don't they come from your desires that battle within you? You desire but do not have, so you kill. You covet but you cannot get what you want, so you quarrel and fight. You do not have because you do not ask God. When you ask, you do not receive, because you ask with wrong motives, that you may spend what you get on your pleasures.

You adulterous people, don't you know that friendship with the world means enmity against God? Therefore, anyone who chooses to be a friend of the world becomes an enemy of God. Or do you think Scripture says without reason that he jealously longs for the spirit he has caused to dwell in us? But he gives us more grace. That is why Scripture says: "God opposes the proud but shows favor to the humble."

Submit yourselves, then, to God. Resist the devil, and he will flee from you. Come near to God and he will come near to you. Wash your hands, you sinners, and purify your hearts, you double-minded.

BLESSED ARE THE POOR IN SPIRIT

REFLECTION

Being poor in spirit means recognizing our need for God. Those areas where we feel the weakest, the most helpless, or ashamed are actually opportunities to draw near to God and rely on his strength. In this way, God turns the bad into good! Find a place to pray and reflect on areas where you need God's help. Write down the top five things you are depending on the Lord for. If you struggle to come up with answers, you can use the prompts below.

At school, I am depending on God to help me _____.

At home, I am depending on God to help me _____.

In my heart, I am depending on God to help me _____.

With my friends, I am depending on God to help me _____.

In life, I am depending on God to help me_____.

SESSION 2:
THOSE WHO MOURN

SESSION SNAPSHOT

Weekly Verses: Matthew 5:4; James 4:7-10

Session Objective: To help students understand the blessing of God's presence in seasons of mourning.

OPENER

Share with students the following definition of the word *mourning*: **"a period of time during which signs of grief are shown." Then, read each situation listed below and ask your group how they might feel after each circumstance.**

- Saying goodbye to a friend who is moving far away

- Getting fired from a job

- Having to put a beloved family pet down

- Losing a loved one

- Waiting for a dream to come to pass

Next, move on to the following question:

- Are there other types of situations that might cause mourning? If so, what are they?

Understanding Matthew 5:4

When Jesus said, "Blessed are those who mourn," he may have been referring to mourning of several different kinds. Some people believe Jesus was talking about Israel mourning for their sins, while others believe he was talking about grieving a personal loss or loved one. Still others think Jesus was talking about the mourning that occurs when a believer suffers for their faith. Regardless of the reason for our mourning, we find a great assurance in his promise to comfort us. He will be nearby. He will mend our hearts and lives. He will relieve our sorrow—for sin, suffering, and loss.

Understanding James 4:7-10

Submission is saying to God, "Not my will, but your will be done." That means surrendering our lives and wills to God through the power of the Holy Spirit. The more we submit to God and draw closer to him, the more we are aware of our own spiritual condition—but also more aware of his grace! In this way, sorrow for sin isn't scary or as difficult as it seems. Rather, sorrow is an important step of faith we take, knowing that forgiveness is already ours in Christ Jesus. God blesses and comforts those who recognize their sin and, with godly sorrow, turn away from disobedience and toward him.

OPENING THE WORD

Ask a student to read Matthew 5:4.

Share with students the different types of mourning Jesus may have been talking about:

1. Mourning our sins and spiritual condition

2. Mourning persecution/suffering for the gospel

3. Mourning the loss of someone or something we love

Discuss the following questions:

- What images or emotions come to mind when you hear the word "mourning?"

- Do you feel it is too narrow of an understanding to define "mourning" in just one way? Could it have to do with grief over loss and grief over sin?

- God mercifully welcomes his children with open arms. How does knowing that make it easier for us to look honestly at our sin?

- Have you ever mourned the loss of something or someone? How did you experience God's comfort in that season?

Ask a student to read James 4:7-10. Discuss the following questions:

- What do you think submission to God means?

- Have you ever mourned over a sin? How did you experience God's comfort?

- Why is it necessary for us to mourn sin and humble ourselves before God? In what ways does God lift up the humble?

UNDERSTANDING THE LARGER STORY

Read the following to your students.

Jesus said that those who mourn are blessed because they will be comforted. It is important to recognize that Jesus points ahead from present (blessed are those who mourn) to future (for they *will be* comforted). In the face of the hopelessness that comes with profound loss, Jesus points to a future of hope. However, it's not simply the passing of time that brings comfort. God comes to us right in the middle of our pain to give us a peace that surpasses understanding.

He also brings us comfort when we are convicted of sin. There are times when we realize our sin has turned us cold to God's love, and we feel the weight of having disobeyed or gone our own way. The good news is that those who mourn their sin and turn to God will be lifted up and comforted.

Play the song "Mercy" by Amanda Cook. Invite students to silently reflect on the following questions:

- Are you experiencing some type of grief or mourning in your life?

- Are there things you have done that you realize are wrong and have caused feelings of sorrow?

- Are there areas of your life where you need to feel God's comfort?

REFLECTION

Have students use their student handout for the following activity.

After students read the Brother Lawrence quote on their student handout, give them a few moments to reflect on and respond to the questions that follow on their sheet. When students have finished writing down answers, invite them to share if they are willing.

TAKEAWAY THOUGHT

Jesus is the ultimate comforter. He is not afraid of our sadness, but comes near to us, enters into our pain, and brings us the promise of hope. Scripture says that because Jesus comforts us, we will know how to comfort others. Ask your students to think about someone in their life who may need comfort or encouragement. Invite them to reach out in the coming week.

SESSION 2: THOSE WHO MOURN

 ## THIS WEEK'S SCRIPTURE PASSAGES

Matthew 5:4
Blessed are those who mourn, for they will be comforted.

James 4:7-10
Submit yourselves, then, to God. Resist the devil, and he will flee from you. Come near to God and he will come near to you. Wash your hands, you sinners, and purify your hearts, you double-minded. Grieve, mourn and wail. Change your laughter to mourning and your joy to gloom. Humble yourselves before the Lord, and he will lift you up.

BLESSED ARE THOSE WHO MOURN

Brother Lawrence was a Catholic saint known for his close and joyous relationship with God. Read the following excerpt from his book, *The Practice of the Presence of God*, and answer the reflection questions that follow.

> Yet, I think it is appropriate to tell you how I perceive myself before God, whom I behold as my King. I consider myself as the most wretched of men. I am full of faults, flaws, and weaknesses, and have committed all sorts of crimes against his King. Touched with a sensible regret I confess all my wickedness to him. I ask his forgiveness. I abandon myself in his hands that he may do what he pleases with me.

> My King is full of mercy and goodness. Far from chastising me, he embraces me with love. He makes me eat at his table. He serves me with his own hands and gives me the key to his treasures. He converses and delights himself with me incessantly, in a thousand and a thousand ways. And he treats me in all respects as his favorite. In this way I consider myself continually in his holy presence.

REFLECTION

- Why do you think Brother Lawrence was able to look so boldly and honestly at his past mistakes and former spiritual condition?

- What stood out to you most about Brother Lawrence's description of God's love toward him?

- In what ways has God shown his love to you?

Take a moment to pray. Ask the Holy Spirit to highlight an area where you need forgiveness. Then give it over to God, asking him to reveal his love to you more than ever before.

SESSION 3: THE MEEK

SESSION SNAPSHOT

Weekly Verses: Matthew 5:5; 11:27-30

Session Objective: To help students understand that being meek does not mean being timid or weak but rather having strength under control.

OPENER

Ask students the following question and write down their answers on a dry erase board.

- Think of the great superpowers, famous conquerors, or leaders from history. What are some of the characteristics they share?

After you have given students the chance to respond, say: "Most of you didn't think of words like 'gentle' or 'meek' to describe the famous leaders of the world. And yet, Jesus says, 'Blessed are the meek, for they will inherit the earth' (Matthew 5:5). So, let's dig into Jesus' words today and find out more about what he is promising to us."

Understanding Matthew 5:5

The word "meek" in the Greek translation meant "mild" or "gentle." It was often used to denote gentle friendliness. Matthew is the only Gospel writer to use the term. He was also the only disciple who worked for Rome collecting taxes. Matthew appears to be interested in highlighting the ways Jesus' values contrasted those of his former employer, Rome.

The reason this third beatitude about meekness attracts so much attention is because it seems to contradict history and experience. Perhaps because "meek" rhymes with "weak," some erroneously conclude that meekness is weakness. However, meekness is a blend of spiritual poise and strength.

Understanding Matthew 11:27-30

For some, religious duties can become a labor, a duty—a burden. Jesus invites his followers to see the truth, come to him, and find rest. This invitation is for everyone. This is not rest from physical labor, but a spiritual refreshing. Rather than the "Pharisaical" approach to following the law, Jesus invites his followers to learn from him and be gentle and humble of heart. Jesus is not saying that following him does not require obedience or effort; rather, they will find Jesus' guidance and presence in their lives if they submit themselves to his guidance and leading through the power of the Holy Spirit.

OPENING THE WORD

Ask a student to read Matthew 5:5.

Share with students that the word "meek" (*praeis*) appears three other times in the New Testament and is translated as "gentle." This word in the Greek was used to describe a broken colt, a gentle breeze, and soothing medicine—all things that point to strength under control. A horse or colt, for example, is a strong animal. Wind is extremely powerful. Medicine can work wonders. When Jesus uses this word, he is talking about strength that is submitted to God, and therefore used for good.

Discuss the following questions:

- What do you think of when you hear the term "meek?"

- Why do you think that meekness is commonly confused with weakness?

- In what ways does it take more strength to be kind rather than hostile?

- In what ways was Jesus gentle? What does it mean for Jesus' followers to be gentle?

Ask a student to read Matthew 11:27-30. Discuss the following questions:

- What stands out the most to you in the passage we just read?

- What are things that can feel heavy either in life or spirituality?

- How do we take on Jesus' yoke?

UNDERSTANDING THE LARGER STORY

Read the following to your students.

Search Scripture and you'll find that Matthew 5 isn't the first mention of the meek inheriting the earth. Psalm 37 states "the meek will inherit the land," a reference to the Israelites entering the Promised Land. An inheritance is something to be received and accepted rather than taken. God's people do not need to conquer the earth. They receive it as an inheritance from God, waiting upon the Lord to drive out their enemies. In this way, we see how meekness also refers to attributes of patience and dependence on God.

Ask a student to read Psalm 37:5-11.

REFLECTION

Have students use their student handout for the following activity.

The next activity is an exercise in practicing Psalm 37:7, which says, "Be still before the Lord and wait patiently for him." Have students grab their handout and disperse to various parts of the room. They can sit on the floor or in chairs, whatever is most comfortable. Walk them through an exercise of silence. Encourage them to concentrate on their breathing, quiet their hearts before God, and listen for the Holy Spirit. It may feel uncomfortable for students at first, but let them know that's okay! (Note: Playing soft, soothing music in the background may be beneficial for this activity.) When students are finished with the exercise, ask them to answer the questions on their student handout.

TAKEAWAY THOUGHT

Today we learned that meekness is not a form of weakness, but quite the opposite! Meekness represents strength under control and a yielding to God. Forms of meekness include gentleness, humility, and the willingness to wait on the Lord.

SESSION 3:
THE MEEK

 ## THIS WEEK'S SCRIPTURE PASSAGES

Matthew 5:5
"Blessed are the meek, for they will inherit the earth."

Matthew 11:27-30
"All things have been committed to me by my Father. No one knows the Son except the Father, and no one knows the Father except the Son and those to whom the Son chooses to reveal him. Come to me, all you who are weary and burdened, and I will give you rest. Take my yoke upon you and learn from me, for I am gentle and humble in heart, and you will find rest for your souls. For my yoke is easy and my burden is light."

BLESSED ARE THE MEEK

Psalm 37:7 says, "Be still before the Lord and wait patiently for him." Stillness and patience are one form of meekness we are learning about this week. As your leader guides you through an exercise of silence, ask God if there's anything he wants to speak to you. Use the white space below to capture anything the Lord might be laying on your heart.

REFLECTION

- How did it feel to be quiet before God? Was it easy? Challenging? Surprising in any way?

- How could you begin to incorporate moments of silence into your schedule?

- Is there anything you are having to patiently wait on God for?

- In what ways is God patient with us?

- Why is it so difficult to wait? How does waiting develop us as Christians?

SESSION 4: THE RIGHTEOUS AND MERCIFUL

SESSION SNAPSHOT

Weekly Verses: Matthew 5:6-7; Luke 6:32-36

Session Objective: To help students understand righteousness as being in right relationship or standing with God.

OPENER

Ask students to fill in the blank: "In my family, we _____." (Examples: In my family, we watch Star Wars. In my family, we love steak dinners. In my family, we play football.) Take turns going around the room sharing until each student has answered.

Share that this lesson is about righteousness, which above all means being in right standing with God. Jesus says that we should want a right relationship with the Father so much that we actually hunger and thirst for it. When we receive Jesus as Lord and Savior, his Spirit in us causes us to hunger and thirst for God. In addition, we also join God's family and become immersed in the family dynamic. What does it look like to be in God's family? Read Luke 6:32-36 and find out! He says those who are kind to their enemies, generous with those who cannot repay them, and do good to all will be called God's "children" because as a Father he is all of those things, too.

Understanding Matthew 5:6-7

Righteousness is first and foremost a right relationship with God. Those who live in a right relationship with God express that by living in right relationships with those around them. Righteousness cannot be achieved apart from an active right relationship with God and others. Jesus said that the blessing for those who hunger and thirst after righteousness is that they will be filled.

Just as God gives us mercy, we must extend mercy to others. Being "merciful" conjures the idea of generosity, forgiveness, and compassion. People show mercy because they have been shown mercy by God. We may not receive mercy from others in return, but we can rest in the fact that God will show us mercy.

Understanding Luke 6:32-36

We are to follow the example of the Father and love, forgive, and show mercy as he does. With this command comes a promise: "You will be children of the Most High." Luke 6 is about God inviting us into the family culture, which is one of outrageous love and mercy.

OPENING THE WORD

Ask a student to read Matthew 5:6-7.

Share with students that in Jesus' day, hunger was a widely shared experience, just as it is in parts of the world today. Jesus used the universal experience of hunger and thirst in the fourth beatitude to announce that those who hunger and thirst for righteousness will be filled. This definitely would have gotten the crowd's attention! So, the question is, what is this righteousness Jesus is talking about—and how is it so fulfilling? Oftentimes, it's easy to confuse righteousness with law-keeping, being "good," or checking off all the right boxes. But this isn't how righteousness is used in the Bible. Instead, righteousness refers to our standing with God in Christ Jesus. This relationship truly does satisfy our deepest hunger and thirst.

Discuss the following questions:

- What does it mean to be in right relationship with God? What does it mean to be in right relationship with others?

- In what ways does focusing on our actions alone fall short of making us righteous?

- We are also talking about mercy today. In what ways are righteous living and being merciful related?

Ask a student to read Luke 6:32-36. Discuss the following questions:

- What is the message of these verses?

- What does it mean to be merciful to others?

- According to verse 36, why are we to be merciful?

- In what ways has God been merciful to you?

UNDERSTANDING THE LARGER STORY

Read the following to your students.

When people ask what they must do to be righteous, the answer is to be in right standing with God through Jesus Christ. He alone is our righteousness. Righteousness is a matter of being, not just doing. He fills us with his Spirit and empowers us to be in right relationship with himself and those around us. We can actually begin to do more of the right things—but not by focusing on outward actions or trying to earn God's favor. Instead, our righteousness is an overflow of God's presence in us.

REFLECTION

Have students use their student handout for the following activity.

Read 2 Corinthians 5:21 to your students. Explain that because of this Scriptural promise, we can confidently say, "I am the righteousness of God in Christ Jesus!" Ask students to search through the Bible and come up with five other "I am" statements that are meaningful to them. They should write their answers on their student handout.

TAKEAWAY THOUGHT

As long as we look at righteousness in terms of perfectionism, we will never grow into a trusting relationship with God. Instead, knowing we are righteous in Christ gives us permission to be authentic with God and brings us into a real relationship with him. Get real before the Lord this week and confess parts of your heart you've been holding back.

SESSION 4:
THE RIGHTEOUS AND MERCIFUL

 ## THIS WEEK'S SCRIPTURE PASSAGES

Matthew 5:6-7
"Blessed are those who hunger and thirst for righteousness, for they will be filled. Blessed are the merciful, for they will be shown mercy."

Luke 6:32-36
"If you love those who love you, what credit is that to you? Even sinners love those who love them. And if you do good to those who are good to you, what credit is that to you? Even sinners do that. And if you lend to those from whom you expect repayment, what credit is that to you? Even sinners lend to sinners, expecting to be repaid in full. But love your enemies, do good to them, and lend to them without expecting to get anything back. Then your reward will be great, and you will be children of the Most High, because he is kind to the ungrateful and wicked. Be merciful, just as your Father is merciful."

BLESSED ARE THE RIGHTEOUS AND MERCIFUL

REFLECTION

After reading 2 Corinthians 5:21, we can confidently say, "I am the righteousness of God in Christ Jesus!" Search through the Bible and come up with five other "I am" statements that are meaningful to you. Write them below.

I am _____ (verse reference:)

I am _____ (verse reference:)

I am _____ (verse reference:)

I am _____ (verse reference:)

I am _____ (verse reference:)

SESSION 5:
THE PURE IN HEART

SESSION SNAPSHOT

Weekly Verses: Matthew 5:8; 1 John 3:1-6

Session Objective: To understand what purity of the heart means.

Supplies: Sheets of white paper, markers, colored pencils.

OPENER

Share with students that catharsis is something that provides relief and allows you to express or purge your emotions. An example of a cathartic activity would be crying if you're sad or working out if you need to release energy.

Ask your students the following question:

- What kinds of activities do people do as catharsis?

Once students have gone around the room and given answers, explain that today's lesson is about purity. The word "purity" in the Bible is the root word for "catharsis." In a catharsis, people purge pent-up anger, grief, and fear that have imprisoned them. A catharsis never sweeps things under the rug or adds a fresh coat of paint. There is nothing surface about a cathartic purification process. It begins at the center and purges everything that is impure.

In today's beatitude "blessed are the pure in heart," Jesus is talking about hearts that have been purged and purified by him. He then promises that those who allow him to purge their hearts will be made pure and holy, and welcomed into his beautiful presence.

Understanding Matthew 5:8

Those who are pure in heart are morally upright, honest, and genuine—devoted to God and his Word. While this is true, being pure in heart is never something we are supposed to accomplish on our own. However, it is possible to live a pure life in Christ! As our hearts are transformed by God's presence, we will find we want to serve and honor God by living pure lives from the inside out.

Understanding 1 John 3:1-6

Great is the love that God has lavished (poured out) on us. As believers, we are children of God. Being his children means that we do not belong to the world, but to God. Because the world does not know God, they will not understand the follower's relationship with God. Our hope is that someday we will see Christ, but as we wait in anticipation, we are to live our lives free from the corruption of sin through purifying power of the Holy Spirit, following the example of Christ.

Sin separates us from God. If we are living for God, we cannot live in sin. We must live in obedience to God, forsaking the sinful life we have repented of. We cannot say we know God if we keep sinning. Living like Christ means turning our backs on sin and allowing the Holy Spirit to lead and empower our lives.

OPENING THE WORD

Ask a student to read Matthew 5:8. Discuss the following questions:

- What attributes flow from hearts that God has made pure?

- Is it possible to have (seemingly) purity of action, but impurity of the heart?

- Why do you think purity of the heart is part of the Beatitudes?

Ask a student to read 1 John 3:1-6. Discuss the following questions:

- The Scripture says God "lavished" love on us by making us his children. What kinds of benefits, gifts, and responsibilities come with becoming a child of God?

- Verse 2 says that when we see Jesus as he is, we will be like him. How does fixing our eyes on Jesus bring us purity?

- What is the promise given to us in this passage about being free from sin?

UNDERSTANDING THE LARGER STORY

Read the following to your students.

When Jesus came to earth, he not only set the standard for purity with the way he lived, he also told his disciples in very clear language that our hearts should be pure. In the culture Jesus was raised in, Jews focused on eating pure foods, living with pure actions, and being ceremonially pure for worship. And yet Jesus declared that the people who would see God are "the pure in heart" (Matthew 5:8). He did not say, "Blessed are the ceremonially pure, the pure in diet, and those who purely keep the law." External actions are much easier to observe and measure than the purity of a heart. To Jesus, the heart was not just a beating organ in one's chest. It is who a person really is and the center of choice, commitment, and will. It is who a person is in the truest sense.

Jesus knew that no one was pure of heart on their own. But instead of saying, "Kiss your dreams of seeing God goodbye," he offered hope. In the original language of Matthew, "The pure in heart" actually means, "Those with hearts that have been purified." None of us is pure before God. But because Jesus died to purify our hearts, we can now approach the throne of God and look upon our Father face to face. Everything that follows flows from hearts that God has made pure.

REFLECTION

Have students use their student handout for the following activity. Read the paragraph below and ask students to answer the questions on their handout.

In today's culture, it can feel extra challenging to keep our hearts pure. If we focus on a long list of "no's" (don't do this; don't do that), we will fail to be pure. Instead, purity is found in one single "yes" to Jesus. We will be pure when we see him as he is, as 1 John 3:2 tells us. When we live in him, we cannot continue to sin.

- What are the challenges of living a pure life in the current culture?

- Often, we spend a lot of time looking at our phones, computers, and game systems. How can we clear our schedules and make time to gaze upon Jesus this week?

- How do you feel you become pure when you see Jesus as he is?

TAKEAWAY THOUGHT

Scripture promises that when we have a pure heart, we will see God. That's a big deal! Ask students to watch for ways that God reveals himself to them this week. Have them carry a journal and make a list of God sightings throughout the week.

SESSION 5:
THE PURE IN HEART

 THIS WEEK'S SCRIPTURE PASSAGES

Matthew 5:8
"Blessed are the pure in heart, for they will see God."

1 John 3:1-6
See what great love the Father has lavished on us, that we should be called children of God! And that is what we are! The reason the world does not know us is that it did not know him. Dear friends, now we are children of God, and what we will be has not yet been made known. But we know that when Christ appears, we shall be like him, for we shall see him as he is. All who have this hope in him purify themselves, just as he is pure. Everyone who sins breaks the law; in fact, sin is lawlessness. But you know that he appeared so that he might take away our sins. And in him is no sin. No one who lives in him keeps on sinning. No one who continues to sin has either seen him or known him.

BLESSED ARE THE PURE IN HEART

REFLECTION

In today's culture, it can feel extra challenging to keep our hearts pure. If we focus on a long list of "no's" (don't do this; don't do that), we will fail to be pure. Instead, purity is found in one single "yes" to Jesus. We will be pure when we see him as he is, as 1 John 3:2 tells us. When we live in him, we cannot continue to sin.

- What are the challenges of living a pure life in the current culture?

- Often, we spend a lot of time looking at our phones, computers, and game systems. How can we clear our schedules and make time to gaze upon Jesus this week?

- How do you feel you become pure when you see Jesus as he is?

SESSION 6: THE PEACEMAKERS

SESSION SNAPSHOT

Weekly Verses: Matthew 5:9; Romans 12:9-21

Session Objective: To help students understand that we are to be peacemakers amidst strife.

OPENER

Write the word "peace" on a dry erase board. Invite students to take a few moments and reflect on the word. Then, ask the group to respond by asking them what comes to mind when they hear and see the word "peace." Write their answers on the board.

Follow up by asking:

- How would you define "peace?"

- If peace is better than conflict, why isn't our world more peaceful than it appears to be today?

- In what ways do we receive God's peace? In what ways can we share God's peace?

Understanding Matthew 5:9

Jesus is the "Prince of Peace" (Isaiah 9:6). Jesus came to bring the ultimate peace between God and humankind (Ephesians 2:14-18). As his followers, we are called to be peacemakers. This means that we are to be peaceful in our spirit and to seek to make peace in our world. Those who make peace in the name of Jesus reflect the character of the Father and are called the children of God.

Understanding Romans 12:9-21

Paul writes that we are to love—and love sincerely. Sincere love requires action. He gives us examples such as *cling to good, devote yourselves to others, share and practice hospitality*. He also tells us to live at peace with everyone. We cannot force others to live at peace, but we can do our part to practice peace in the world. If we live out the actions mentioned in these verses, we will lay a foundation for peace within our relationships. Paul's instructions for practicing "love in action" open the door for Christians to sow peace.

OPENING THE WORD

Ask a student to read Matthew 5:9.

Share with students that Jesus wanted his audience to understand what he meant by making peace so much that he elaborated on it a few verses later.

Ask a student to read Matthew 5:21-23.

Let's reflect for a moment. Jesus valued peace to the extent that he even said it should be prioritized over worship. Wow—that's hard to imagine! Another thing Jesus emphasizes here is our need to actively pursue peace. Sometimes in conflict the tendency can be for us to pity ourselves and our circumstances, or to let bitterness and hatred grow toward another person. Instead of focusing on how we've been hurt, Jesus calls his followers to be conscious of how their actions may have hurt others. Peacemakers take the first step.

Discuss the following questions:

- What does it mean to be a peacemaker?

- In what ways does being a believer mean we cultivate peace within our relationships? Does it mean we never stand up for what we believe or always appease others? If not, what does it mean?

- Is there anyone who might have something against you? What is the first step in making peace?

Ask a student to read Romans 12:9-21. Discuss the following questions:

- What is sincere love like? What is insincere love like?

- According to this passage, how can we cultivate peace in our relationships with others?

- Of all the commands listed in these verses, which one is most challenging to you?

UNDERSTANDING THE LARGER STORY

Read the following to your students.

During Jesus' ministry, he often talked about a new kingdom. He also declared himself the Messiah, which meant he was to rule over Israel. In a time when Rome occupied Jerusalem and the Romans were famous for believing that peace was achieved only through war, Jesus' words would have gotten a lot of people's attention. In fact, there's a chance that many in the crowd came to hear Jesus' Sermon on the Mount just because they were asking themselves, "Is he the one who will end Rome's domination?"

Of course, now we know that Jesus came to earth to accomplish much more than overthrowing Rome or being Israel's king. He is enthroned over all the earth! Not only that, but in Isaiah 9:6 we read about what type of ruler Jesus is: the Prince of Peace.

So what does peace look like to God? In contrast to the Roman view that peace was inseparably linked to war, Psalm 85 presents a strikingly different view. Peace is God's gift to his people—something received and not taken by force.

Read Psalm 85:7-13 to your students. Discuss the following questions:

- Which definition of peace—the Roman one or Jesus'—feels more familiar in our world? Why?

- How do most people resolve conflict? How does God want us to resolve conflict?

- In what ways does inner peace affect our ability to be a peacemaker in the world?

- What are the barriers to living out peace in your life?

REFLECTION

Have students use their student handout for the following activity.

Romans 12:9-21 gives us a picture of many ways we can be peacemakers. Divide students into groups and ask them to re-read the Romans 12 passage. On the left-hand side of their student handout, students will write down a list of all the different examples of making peace that are found in the passage. On the right-hand side, students will translate these examples into relevant, current language. (For example: "love sincerely" might translate to "love without having secret agendas," and "be devoted to one another" might translate to "be a loyal friend and don't talk smack on others.")

TAKEAWAY THOUGHT

Today we learned that peace is a gift from God, but also that it sometimes requires us to take a first step toward reconciliation with others. Ask students to consider who the Lord might be asking them to reach out to this week in a spirit of reconciliation.

SESSION 6:
THE PEACEMAKERS

 ## THIS WEEK'S SCRIPTURE PASSAGES

Matthew 5:9
"Blessed are the peacemakers, for they will be called children of God."

Romans 12:9-21
Love must be sincere. Hate what is evil; cling to what is good. Be devoted to one another in love. Honor one another above yourselves. Never be lacking in zeal, but keep your spiritual fervor, serving the Lord. Be joyful in hope, patient in affliction, faithful in prayer. Share with the Lord's people who are in need. Practice hospitality.

Bless those who persecute you; bless and do not curse. Rejoice with those who rejoice; mourn with those who mourn. Live in harmony with one another. Do not be proud, but be willing to associate with people of low position. Do not be conceited.

Do not repay anyone evil for evil. Be careful to do what is right in the eyes of everyone. If it is possible, as far as it depends on you, live at peace with everyone. Do not take revenge, my dear friends, but leave room for God's wrath, for it is written: "It is mine to avenge; I will repay," says the Lord. On the contrary: "If your enemy is hungry, feed him; if he is thirsty, give him something to drink. In doing this, you will heap burning coals on his head." Do not be overcome by evil, but overcome evil with good.

BLESSED ARE THE PEACEMAKERS

REFLECTION

Romans 12:9-21 gives us a picture of many ways we can be peacemakers. Re-read the passage in your group. On the left-hand side of your student handout, write down a list of all the different examples of making peace that are found in the passage. On the right-hand side, translate these examples into relevant, current language. (For example: "love sincerely" might translate to "love without having secret agendas," and "be devoted to one another" might translate to "be a loyal friend and don't talk smack on others.")

This activity should be fun—so get creative with your translations!

SESSION 7:
THE PERSECUTED

SESSION SNAPSHOT

Weekly Verses: Matthew 5:10-12; 2 Timothy 3:12-15

Session Objective: To understand the blessing in being persecuted for Jesus.

Supplies Needed: Congregational candles

OPENER

Ask students to name some of the things that make Christians different from the rest of the world. Write the list on a dry erase board.

Understanding Matthew 5:10-12

Jesus let his followers know that they should not be shocked if they experience persecution because of their relationship with him. Our righteousness (right relationship or standing with God) is not a neutral stance, and it's often offensive to nonbelievers. Because the world does not understand the ways of God, believers who live contrary to the ways of this world are targeted as enemies. Believers are to rejoice and be glad in light of their heavenly reward.

Understanding 2 Timothy 3:12-15

Paul tells Timothy that followers who live in obedience to God will experience persecution. Paul knew firsthand the suffering that comes from a life lived for God (Acts 14:22). He encourages Timothy to continue to believe what he has learned from Scripture and live it daily. The Word of God coupled with his relationship with Christ would sustain him during any difficulties he might face.

OPENING THE WORD

Ask a student to read Matthew 5:10-12.

Share with students that Jesus considered it important to prepare his followers for the difficulties ahead. He wanted to make sure his listeners understood the high cost of kingdom citizenship. He even changed his language from "Blessed are they" to "Blessed are *you*." He made this beatitude personal, speaking directly to his audience. Jesus warned they would receive insults, experience physical abuse, and have their reputations damaged by gossip.

Discuss the following questions:

- What does it mean to be persecuted for our righteousness?

- Have you ever experienced persecution for your faith?

- Why do you think the gospel tends to flourish in areas of the world that are under extreme persecution?

- Why do you think Jesus changed the form of the last beatitude to address the crowd directly?

- What should our attitude be when we experience persecution? Why?

Ask a student to read 2 Timothy 3:12-15. Discuss the following questions:

- Paul tells Timothy that "everyone who wants to live a godly life in Christ Jesus will be persecuted." Why do you think being a Christian is so controversial?

- In what ways does living the Jesus way put us at odds with culture?

- According to verses 14-15, what does Paul tell Timothy to continue to do? Why?

- In what ways does God's Word and our relationship with him help us persevere in our faith, especially during times of persecution?

UNDERSTANDING THE LARGER STORY

Read the following to your students.

The kingdom of God is exactly that—a kingdom. Many times, God's kingdom is in stark contrast to the kingdoms and ways of the world, and because Jesus is anointed as the Son of God, he is a threat to every other power and principality. He is a lightning rod. He is a person the world cannot feel neutral toward, but instead will love or hate (though Scripture says all will ultimately bow down before him).

Jesus spoke directly to his disciples and the crowd before him, blessing those who would experience persecution. During a time of harsh, oppressive Roman rule, Jesus knew some standing among him would be killed for their beliefs. Even now you can see what remains of the Roman Coliseum, where tens of thousands of Christians chose to die rather than to deny Jesus. And while the kingdom of Rome tried to go head-to-head with the kingdom of heaven that Jesus announced, Rome stands in ruins today, but Jesus' Word continues to grow in power and influence. Jesus' kingdom is always victorious. His kingdom always endures.

While persecution is never a blessing, God acts on behalf of his persecuted people. In the midst of persecution, God is at work, blessing those who experience persecution, slander, hatred, and even death for the sake of Christ and his kingdom. In addition to receiving God's blessings in the here and now, there is an even greater reward in heaven for those who ultimately persevere.

REFLECTION

Have students use their student handout for the following activity.

Divide students into groups and ask them to pray for the persecuted church around the world. Then have students write a letter to an anonymous martyr—someone who has lost their life for the gospel. This martyr may never have had their story told in a book or a statue created to commemorate their sacrifice. Instead, this martyr may have been killed for Jesus and no one will ever know. But God knows and sees. Take some time to write a private thank you note to this martyr. You can share with your group if you'd like, but you don't have to.

TAKEAWAY THOUGHT

As believers who have decided to follow Jesus even when it's not popular, we understand being excluded at times. Do you know of anyone at your school or church who might feel lonely or like an outsider—either by intentional or unintentional exclusion? What can you do to offer support, get involved in their life, and make things better?

SESSION 7:
THE PERSECUTED

 ## THIS WEEK'S SCRIPTURE PASSAGES

Matthew 5:10-12
"Blessed are those who are persecuted because of righteousness, for theirs is the kingdom of heaven. Blessed are you when people insult you, persecute you and falsely say all kinds of evil against you because of me. Rejoice and be glad, because great is your reward in heaven, for in the same way they persecuted the prophets who were before you."

2 Timothy 3:12-15
In fact, everyone who wants to live a godly life in Christ Jesus will be persecuted, while evildoers and impostors will go from bad to worse, deceiving and being deceived. But as for you, continue in what you have learned and have become convinced of, because you know those from whom you learned it, and how from infancy you have known the Holy Scriptures, which are able to make you wise for salvation through faith in Christ Jesus.

BLESSED ARE THE PERSECUTED

REFLECTION

Write a letter to an anonymous martyr—someone who has lost their life for the gospel. This martyr may never have had their story told in a book or a statue created to commemorate their sacrifice. Instead, this martyr may have been killed for Jesus and no one will ever know. But God knows and sees. Take some time to write a private thank-you note to this martyr. You can share with your group if you'd like, but you don't have to.

_____

_____

_____

_____

_____

_____

_____

_____